School Board Talk!

The Art of Effective Communication

Cheli Cerra, M.Ed. & Ruth Jacoby, Ed.D.

JOSSEY-BASS
A Wiley Imprint
www.josseybass.com

Published by Jossey-Bass
A Wiley Imprint
989 Market Street, San Francisco, CA 94103-1741   www.josseybass.com

Jossey-Bass books and products are available through most bookstores. To contact
Jossey-Bass directly call our Customer Care Department within the U.S. at 800-956-7739,
outside the U.S. at 317-572-3986 or fax 317-572-4002.

Jossey-Bass also publishes its books in a variety of electronic formats. Some content that
appears in print may not be available in electronic books.

ISBN 0-7879-7912-0

Printed in the United States of America
FIRST EDITION
PB Printing   10   9   8   7   6   5   4   3   2   1

The Buzz About *School Board Talk!*

"School Board Talk! *presents a series of constructive suggestions school board members can use when communicating in their role as a board member. Each vignette deals with areas specifically pertaining to members' responsibilities in carrying out their governance duties on a school board. This book should be particularly helpful to new school board members.*"

James R. Oglesby, Ph. D.
Past President
National School Boards Association

"School Board Talk! *offers simple advice for a complex job. It is 'must' reading for anyone who wears or wants to wear the mantel of a school board member.*"

Dr. Wayne Blanton, *Executive Director*
Florida School Boards Association

"School Board Talk! The Art of Effective Communication *offers practical tips on being an effective school board member that translate into sound advice for all those who devote their time and energy to helping the nation's school children.*"

Michael Eader, *Executive Director*
Florida Association of School Administrators

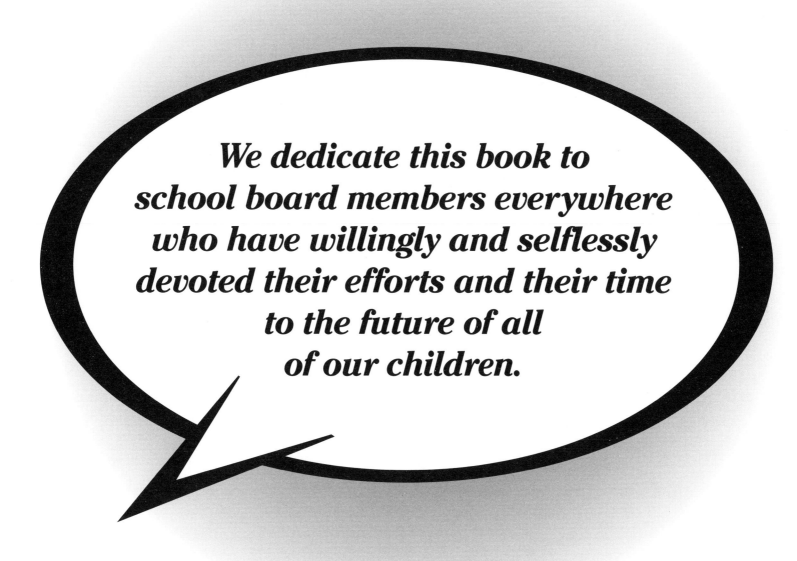

Table of Contents

Appendix A

Toolkit for Success

How to Use This Book

School Board Talk! offers some practical advice on surviving as a school board member. It provides more than 50 "down-to-earth" situations in the form of "snapshots" that both new and veteran members may encounter during their school board careers. Each snapshot is accompanied by one or more **"tips"** on how you might handle the situation.

School Board Talk! also adds some sage advice designed to help brighten your decision-making process and, hopefully, give you a smile. The snapshots represent only a sampling of the hundreds of circumstances in which you may find yourself as a school board member. The accompanying **"tips"** on how to handle each event can be applied to many different situations. The authors interviewed many of your peers in an effort to make sure the information they present is relevant to your job. The result is this collection of very short stories that deal with very real occurrences.

The book also provides a series of worksheets designed to help you in your political career by enabling you to keep careful records of the public side of your public life.

In researching the book, the authors quickly recognized that the nation's 95,000 school board members are dedicated and energized people who have accepted one of the toughest political assignments in existence and one of the most important ones.

Like you, they have willingly agreed to be entrusted with every parent's most cherished possession and with the nation's most valuable resource—our children.

www.School-talk.com

The Genesis of School Boards

"Next in importance to freedom and justice is popular education, without which neither freedom nor justice can be permanently maintained."

James A. Garfield

The Genesis of School Boards
A BRIEF HISTORY

Your school board office predates the birth of the nation itself. Its genesis is in colonial New England where citizens at their town hall meetings dealt with school matters as they grappled with a host of other governmental-type decisions.

Eventually, the responsibility for school administration became part of the job of the town's elected selectmen who handled all the administrative functions for the colonists. The job of running the school expanded and became more time-consuming as the towns and their populations grew. The selectmen turned to appointed temporary school committees to oversee the schools. Ultimately the temporary committees evolved into continuing committees, which were the forerunners of today's school boards.

In 1826, Massachusetts took the final step toward creation of today's modern school boards by ordering each of its towns to elect a permanent committee specifically to take charge of the public schools. (In Massachusetts, the term "school committee" continues to be in use.) Throughout the evolution, the concept of school governance was founded on keeping it responsive to the local citizenry and as close to home as possible.

Today, more than 368 years since the first New England colonists began making decisions about their schools at town meetings, local school boards strive to do the same in much the same forum, which basically is an open meeting where any citizen has the opportunity to have his voice heard on school issues.

Introduction

> "Twenty years from now you will be more disappointed by the things you didn't do than by the ones you did do. So throw off the bowlines. Sail away from the safe harbor. Catch the trade winds in your sails. Explore. Dream. Discover."
>
> **Mark Twain**

Introduction

Public school board members in the United States cannot be spotted in a line-up. There is no common unique physical characteristic that distinguishes the 95,000 board members from non–school board members. To the ordinary member of the public, you might be the neighbor next door; the man standing in line at the supermarket checkout; the mother steering her teenage daughter through the mall; a local businessman; a retired teacher or a former school administrator.

Across the country, you reflect the multiethnic population that makes up the United States. You come in all shapes and sizes. Within your ranks there are tall, short, and average height people and thin, stocky, and athletic looking specimens. You run the gamut of all ages: some as young as the early twenties and some long since past being eligible for Medicare.

Most of you—96 percent—are elected; a few are appointed. More than two-thirds of you are not compensated for the job, but receive a small stipend to compensate for some of the expenses associated with the office. You are elected to offices that are sometimes partisan and sometimes non-partisan and your districts may constitute an entire city or county or a portion thereof, commonly referred to as a single member district. Across the nation you fall into the category of "politician." For most of you,

the school board seat may be the only stop on the political career ladder. For others, like former President Jimmy Carter, it may be the first stop in a long career of public service.

You function in rural, suburban, and urban areas and govern huge districts with as many as 200,000 to more than one million students to very small districts with less than 20 students. Some of you shoulder your school board's responsibilities on a fulltime basis; others must juggle the demands of the office with the demands of earning a living.

Together, you and your colleagues serve 47 million public school students in 14,890 school districts.

Your physical appearance may not be unique. What is unique is your commitment to the education of this nation's young people. It is a commitment fraught with controversy and criticism, but it also is a commitment to a continuation of the ideals, hopes, and promises upon which the nation was founded.

You exemplify the concept of government "by the people and for the people," with the added enhancement of "near the people." You operate close to home without the luxury of being able to make decisions miles away in your state capitol or the nation's capitol where travel distances can keep constituents at bay.

In fact, you are besieged by education "experts" on the homefront. Not necessarily by the teachers

Introduction

and school administrators for whom education is a trained profession, but more likely by the neighbor who has a child in school, the business associate who went to school, the retired acquaintance who knows someone who went to school. There exists an endless network of people who have some link to public schools and some opinion on how they should function. As a school board member, you generally fill the most accessible elected office in your community.

You, literally, are on the frontline of the education reform battlefield. Communities, states, and the federal government look to school boards to institute education reforms, some created at the local level, others mandated at the state and federal level. Boards must institute policies that ensure all students can succeed in school and that improve student achievement on a rising scale each year. At the same time, it is up to you and your peers to walk the tightropes between local needs and state mandates, between conflicting state and federal regulations, between limitless needs supported by limited resources.

You do your job as a school board member within a tangle of legal mandates, fiscal restraints, and political realities, which largely become apparent only after you have assumed office.

You operate schools with a "come one, come all" policy and then are subject to criticism from educational entities that are able to select their clientele and limit their offerings.

You are subject to the naysayers who view school board members as superfluous. Across the nation, boards are under fire to increase student achievement, to do more with less, to operate schools like businesses, to compete with each other, as well as with the private sector. In 24 of 50 states, laws now allow for the takeover of districts with poor academic achievement. In several urban districts, mayors are in charge of their school districts' governance and operations. There are demands that large school districts be broken up into smaller ones and that small districts merge with others to maximize resources and reduce duplication.

As a school board member, you are an easy target for criticism. At any given moment, there probably are one or more members of your community upset with the school system and, therefore, upset with you and your colleagues. You can be chastised publicly and privately for all kinds of reasons by all kinds of people: a parent whose child isn't doing as well in school as expected; a community that is not getting fast enough relief for an overcrowded school; a legislator who can't get a constituent's child transferred from one school to another; a teacher who wants a pay raise; an administrator whose work is going unheralded.

Introduction

You also are a focal point for accountability: an elected official who is subject to open government laws and public records laws, numerous audits, citizens' oversight committees, and constant media scrutiny and who is the object of frequent litigation.

The nation's 14,000 plus school boards are an essential part of the American fabric of democracy, providing the bridge between what the community wants for its children and what the schools require from their community. As the fiscal agents for billions of tax dollars, boards are expected to make wise and expeditious spending decisions that meet the public's demands for efficient and effective government.

Your span of direct authority is spelled out in hundreds of state and federal laws. It is a limited span. Board members are authorized to adopt policies for the school district; hire the superintendent if that's an appointed office; hire, fire, and discipline employees but only based on the superintendent's recommendation; collectively bargain or meet and confer with the district's employee groups. Within those general categories, you are called upon to make multitudes of decisions, most based on the superintendent's recommendations, many which bubbled up from you through him or her.

The enormity of your job as a school board member is awesome. The potential for reward is tremendous. Business looks to you to produce qualified workers, and community groups call upon you to create a better quality of life in all corners.

Above all, you are entrusted with parents' most cherished possessions and the nation's most valuable resource—our children.

That's what distinguishes you from the ordinary citizen.

www.school-talk.com

Notes:

Chapter One

Board Panache

"Words are just words
and without heart they
have no meaning."
Chinese proverb

Snapshot #1:

The Learning Curve

www.school-talk.com

Congratulations! You have won the election and now reality begins to set in. So much to learn, so little time, is a familiar refrain bouncing inside a new school board member's head. Governing a school district is so much more than just dealing with what students should learn. There's the:

- **plethora of state rules and regulations;**
- **local school board policies;**
- **procedures for accepting bids;**
- **rules for approving personnel appointments and job descriptions;**
- **budget upon budget decisions;**
- **discipline cases;**
- **ways to deal with the superintendent and staff;**
- **necessity of understanding open meetings and public records laws;**
- **lists of school board ethics and correct protocol;**
- **procedures for accepting purchasing orders;**
- **responsibilities when working with employee groups;**
- **requirements to approve contracts and grant applications;**
- **ins and outs of getting your own items on the board agenda;**
- **who's who of staff; and**
- **seemingly endless lists of programs, policies, and people.**

What should you do?

Ignorance may be bliss; but not when your job is to improve student achievement.

Tip : Turn to the superintendent for help. After all, you are his employer. Ask him to have a notebook prepared for you containing much of the information you need. Review the **Information Checklist** on *page 117,* to get an idea of some of the materials you will find valuable. Ask the superintendent to schedule orientation meetings for you with key staff members so they can explain their roles and responsibilities and talk about some of the programs they oversee. You have taken on a complex and enormously important job so don't be afraid to ask questions. Getting the right information up front can save you a lot of mistakes later.

Seek help. The more you know, the more effective you can be.

Snapshot #2:
The Non-working Work Orders

O n a visit to a school, the principal complains that he can't get the boiler fixed properly. It is constantly breaking down. Sweaters and coats have become as important to the classroom as books and paper. He complains that the district office consistently ignores his work orders. Your inclination is to call the superintendent and demand the maintenance "swat team" be sent in immediately. What should you do?

Tip : School visits are important. They give you the opportunity to see for yourself what life in school is like for the staff and the students. They demonstrate to the staff and students that you "care." They almost always create "to do" lists. School district maintenance work orders seem to replicate like rabbits. As soon as two are completed, six more materialize. It is appropriate to communicate complaints that you hear to the superintendent, but your responsibility is not to micromanage the administration of the schools. Many work orders never quite get completed, get lost in the paper shuffle or routed to the wrong place. When you do speak to the superintendent ask him to let you know why it appears so difficult to get this maintenance problem fixed. You may find out that getting replacement parts for boilers on a timely basis is the problem and that there are similar repair holdups throughout the district. Suggest that, if there is such a pattern, something as simple as stocking most-needed parts could speed up the repair process. Above all remember, your job is to set policy, not to run the school system.

Be prepared to deal with finite resources and infinite needs.

Problems are like puzzles: you need all the pieces to solve them.

Snapshot #3:

Scaling the Paper Mountain

Tip : The paper flow can be overwhelming, particularly for new school board members. The key is to: organize, organize, and organize. Find out how the board office organizes things. Is there one person who will keep a master file for all the members or will you have the luxury of having someone to specifically handle your material? If there is a single, master file for everyone, no need to hang on to your copy of a letter or memo that went to every board member. Toss it. Rely on the master file. If you don't have any office help, take the time to organize your own file system and make it a practice to use it. Once you have handled a piece of paper, don't throw it back in the in-box to look at a second time; put it in your "no need to read again" file or in one that indicates it will need some follow-up action. If the educational jargon in the material slows you down, have patience and ask for help. It's amazing how quickly you will become comfortable with the language of education. Whatever you do, try not to let the paper mountain grow to Mt. Everest heights. Once you do, you'll never be able to scale it.

Your inbox "overfloweth." As quickly as you try to empty it, the paper seems to regenerate itself in the form of agenda items, back-up material, letters to you, copies of letters to other board members, copies of letters to the superintendent, contracts, memos to you from staff, and copies of memos to staff from other staff. It never ends. What should you do?

> **Work smart, not long.**

> **Organizing is the key to winning the paper chase.**

Snapshot #4:
The Unrecognized School Board Member

As a school board member, you want people to see you are interested, active and "out there." You visit schools regularly. On one such visit, you are "stunned" to discover that many of the classroom teachers don't recognize you as a board member. You feel a slight stab of ego-dismay. For one fleeting minute, you think of calling the superintendent and demanding he hold a teacher in-service workshop on "Board Member Recognition." Then you come to your senses and realize the teachers are doing their job and you need to do yours. What should you do?

Tip : Your job is to focus on what you can do to help the school and its staff successfully do their job. "Recognition" may make you feel good, but it won't do one thing to improve student achievement. If you turn your attention to helping the school staff, you can be pretty sure you will be recognized on a future visit.

* JUST A THOUGHT!
For security reasons it is wise to post a picture of the superintendent and school board members in every school.

www.school-talk.com

Treat your ego like a wet umbrella; leave it outside the schoolroom door.

Remember: you've been elected, not anointed.

Snapshot #5:

Pre-planning Your Special Event Role

If you want the spotlight, make sure to insert the fuse.

Prepare in advance for school district events. Surprises are for parties, not public appearances.

The annual "Teacher of the Year" luncheon is a lovely event. You arrive, take your seat at a front table and suddenly realize you have no idea what you are supposed to do, if anything. You anticipate being introduced. If you are not, you will be annoyed, upset, and hurt. After all, these are "your" teachers and this is "your" school district. Maybe you will be asked to say a few words. If so, what will you say? If not, why not? Aren't you worth listening to? What should you do?

Tip : As a board member, it may seem crystal clear to you that being introduced and participating in the program are your due. But don't forget, the event planners have a long list of things to worry about. Have Mrs. Carlson's fourth graders cut, colored and pasted enough paper flowers for a centerpiece on every table? Will the superintendent and school board chairman's presentations be too long? Will the chicken a la orange be better served over rice or under broccoli? What you need to know is whether there will be assigned seating. Will you be introduced? Who should you alert that you are in the room if you are to be introduced? Do you have to make a speech or participate in some other way? Take a few minutes to check it all out in advance before you check in.

Snapshot #6:
The Board Vote You Lose

You've learned about a new reading program, which is having great success. You are convinced that it is the answer to improving student reading at the first and second grade levels. You want the program implemented in every elementary school in your district and you can't imagine why anyone would disagree with your fabulous idea. You place the item for discussion on the next school board agenda. Much to your chagrin, your fellow board members, for a variety of reasons, do not support your item. They vote it down. What should you do?

> *When you "lose," let it go and move on to the next issue; when you "win," remember to say "thank you."*

Tip :

You could spend the next 15 minutes silently pondering how you can be so smart and everyone else on the board so "not smart." You promise yourself when "their" agenda items come up, you will vote "no," even if you support them. Not a good idea. The board's collective action is not directed at you as an individual, but at a concept the members simply did not support. Maybe they are right and you are wrong; maybe it is the other way around, but it doesn't matter. Today your item lost; next month an item of yours may win. The fellow board members you mentally are shooting darts at today may be your winning votes next time.

> *A "no" vote against you is a vote against an idea, not against you.*

Snapshot #7:

The Agenda Crush

As a parent you always were actively involved in school board issues. You attended school board meetings, tried to read the agenda materials, and often addressed the board on behalf of your parents' group. Then you determined you could better use your energies by being a member of the board. You ran for election and won. You quickly found out that you had no idea just how much material you would be required to read. You spend evening after evening just trying to keep up. What should you do?

Tip:

Your responsibility is to read everything so that you can make intelligent decisions about the many issues that require your attention. Don't despair; things will get easier as you get more experienced. Once you have weathered the first year, some of the documents that come across your desk will be second and third generation items, such as contracts that are renewed annually. It won't be necessary for you to plow your way through them word for word, particularly if you ask the superintendent to direct staff to underline any new language that has been added. That technique will help speed your way through some of the paperwork.

> **Be sure to find out which documents you legally are required to read before you can vote on an item.**

> **Experience is the best way to overcome paperwork frustration. Underlining helps too.**

Snapshot #8:

Email Is a Public Domain

Your daily dose of email messages includes one from a parent who says her sixth grader has been molested at school. She is frantic, worried, and anxious that the incident not become the topic of conversation in the school and in the community. She is sure her child is telling the truth. What should you do?

Tip : Caution the parent that, in many instances, school board members' emails are considered public documents so talking to you by telephone or in person would be advisable. Offer to refer the parent to an appropriate staff member immediately, but be aware the sensitive nature of the call may make the parent reluctant to talk to school officials. Be sure you know and understand the procedure to follow for reporting such serious charges. Some states require school officials to report the accusations to the proper authorities.

Handle emails carefully; they are replete with public rights.

View your emails as the public's window to your world.

Snapshot #9:
The Email Deluge

Tip: In this instance, Anne's true best friend may be the mail program's automated response feature. When a board member receives a flood of emails about one issue, the automated response can come to the rescue. The response is automatically triggered when your incoming message has one or more pre-selected key words such as "boundaries."

Use the response as a friendly alter ego. Let it thank the sender for taking the time to be concerned and sharing some thoughts with you. Assure the senders that you carefully consider all the information they've taken the time to send you. A carefully worded automatic response to email messages has its place in the communication venue. For one thing, it never loses its temper and says the wrong thing.

Anne was so excited when she finally learned to use a computer. She couldn't wait to open it every day to see if she received any email messages. But she doesn't feel that way anymore. Since the school board voted to change school boundaries, Anne has become an email queen. Some days she gets 50 to 75 messages. While Anne wants to be a responsible board member and respond to every email, she is starting to view the "delete" button as her best friend. What should she do?

An email response says you care; a lack of response says you don't.

Thoughtfully worded automated email responses are useful communication tools.

Chapter Two:

Peer Points: Building Board Relationships

"The first duty of a leader is to make oneself loved without courting love. To be loved without 'playing up' to anyone—even to himself."

Andre Malraus

Snapshot #10:
The Case of the Missing Peers

The local chapter of the League of Women Voters has chosen you its "Woman of the Year" and will honor you at a formal dinner. You feel exalted and excited, but somewhat miffed to discover that scheduling conflicts will prevent any of your fellow board members from sharing this dramatic event with you. Privately, you think at least some of them could change their plans and celebrate the evening with you. What should you do?

Tip: It's normal to want to share your success with those who share the same venue that brought you the accolades, but try not to take their absence too personally. Some of your peers may want to be at the dinner to applaud your success, but have previous commitments, which prevent their attending. Take action to minimize future scheduling conflicts. Suggest the board members institute a common calendar that lists all the important upcoming commitments. That way it will be possible for board members to better plan their schedules and possibly divide up their attendance when there are several events occurring at one time. In the meantime, sprinkle a few gentle grains of guilt over your fellow board members by displaying your award at the next board meeting and announcing that you could not have earned it "without all their help."

A common calendar can help reduce scheduling conflicts among school board members.

Remember, it's absence that is supposed to make the heart grow fonder, not attendance.

Snapshot #11:
The Board Member Going Solo

You are surprised and angry when you pick up the morning newspaper and read that a fellow board member has announced he intends to privatize the school lunch program. The article quotes the board member as saying that too much of the lunch food is ending up in the garbage. He believes it would be more economical to have vendors provide pizza, burgers, and fried chicken. What should you do?

Tip : The irony is that you happen to support privatization, but it is not your decision alone to make. This would be a major policy change that needs to be studied by the superintendent and brought to the board for discussion. Unfortunately, one board member has opted, instead, to use the media to try to manage the school district. It's not the first time this has happened. To the contrary, it is becoming a pattern. Although you've tried before, continue to try the gentle approach to changing behavior. Invite the board member out for pizza and review with him just how many votes it takes to get a program approved, including those he favors. Remind him that the proper protocol is to bring the issue to the board and ask it to direct the superintendent to examine a proposal and bring a recommendation for board discussion and action. Explain that if his programs are going to succeed, he needs both board consensus and staff and community support. Major changes first should be well thought out, brought to the superintendent, discussed by the stakeholders and then presented to the school board for discussion and action. Don't expect instant change to spring from your rationale discussion and gentle prodding. Be realistic! Accept the fact that changing behavior is a slow process. Be prepared to buy a lot of pizzas.

> *"Boardsmanship" is not a solo sport.*

> *The outhouse is only a few steps down from the penthouse.*

Snapshot #12: The Frequent Flyer

Graham loves to travel and one of the best things he's discovered about being a school board member is that there are all kinds of travel opportunities. He takes flight whenever an out-of-town meeting presents itself. He goes to regional conferences, state conferences, and national events. He attends meetings of curriculum directors and finance officers, of reading specialists and guidance counselors. Find an education-related group, particularly meeting in some enticing geographic area, and chances are you will find Graham. His tourist tendencies are playing havoc with the school board's travel budget. He is using more than his share of this fund and continually sends memos to the superintendent to replenish it. What should you do?

Develop a budget for school board members' travel and adopt ground rules for using the funds and reporting on what was learned at the meeting.

Tip : A school board policy on members' travel procedures can help curtail Graham and other excessive board travelers. The policy can stipulate that, once the board approves the size of the travel budget as part of its budget decisions, the funds must be divided equally among all the board members. Any member who exceeds his allotment will have to place a budget amendment before the board for everyone to see and discuss. That should get some media attention and help clip Graham's frequent flyer wings.

Make sure traveling broadens board knowledge, not bends the board's budget.

Snapshot #13:

A Colleague's Election Campaign

Juan is one of the most experienced members of the board and one of the most outspoken. When Juan believes in something, he has no qualms about casting the lone dissenting vote. He has taken issue with the media, with groups of parents, with fellow board members, and with the local legislative delegation. Juan's position is that he votes his conscience and, if the voters don't like it, they will tell him so at the next election.

Even though you think Juan could be a little less inflexible about his positions, you admire his honesty, forthrightness and convictions. You are upset when he draws re-election opposition. You want to help Juan, but what if his opponent wins? Your support of the losing candidate could cause a major rift on the school board. What should you do?

Tip : Don't stand on the corner waiving placards with Juan's name. Give Juan advice; names of people who will be happy to post his signs and carry his bumper stickers. Share the names of potential campaign contributors who might help him. On Election Day, do the most important thing: "Vote for Juan."

Every board member should be elected on his or her own merits. Getting too involved in a colleague's election has as much chance of leading to school board acrimony as school board accord.

Snapshot #14:
The Careless Comment

Felipe took a break after several hours of student expulsion hearings. Tired and unhappy that, as a school board member, he had to spend so much time on discipline, Felipe idly mused out loud to no one in particular that perhaps the school board should return to the old days when paddling was an accepted form of discipline. A nearby reporter overheard Felipe's remark. The morning's newspaper carried a story that at least one school board member favored corporal punishment. The local television station asked for interviews from board members as to whether they supported paddling and from the superintendent as to whether he would recommend reinstating it as a discipline measure. Parents on both sides of the issue got involved. The media kept the story alive for a week. No one seemed to want to listen to Felipe's follow-up statement that he really did not support paddling, but had just been commenting that something needed to be done to improve student discipline. What should you learn?

No matter how idle your thought may be, it becomes your opinion when you voice it.

www.school-talk.com

Tip : Felipe learned the hard way that he has to curtail his remarks and save the careless comments for the privacy of his shower. When it comes to political life, "Think before you speak," grows from simply being good advice to practically being a commandment.

Believe what you say before you say it.

JUST A THOUGHT! Be careful what you say, all ears are listening.

Snapshot #15:

The Excessively Inquisitive Board Member

Nelson is a school board member with an insatiable need for information. On a daily basis, he issues memos to staff asking for statistical data, documentation, explanations, information, program reviews, evaluations, and "What are we going to do about this?" queries. Nelson knows that staff already carries a major workload, but his inquisitive mind and attention to detail fuels his constant "need-to-know." Although the superintendent has tried to explain the concept of only 24 hours in a day, seven days a week to Nelson, it hasn't helped. Nelson has staff reeling with requests. What should Nelson do?

Have a proper procedure in place for requesting information from and communicating with staff. Recognize a process that starts with the superintendent is a traffic control measure, not a roadblock device.

If you do communicate with staff, copy the superintendent. The superintendent is your employee, not the staff.

Tip : The school board should have a rule detailing how requests for information from school board members are to be handled and stipulating that all of them go through the superintendent to staff. An orderly process for handling board requests for information can help both the staff and the board members. For the former, it can provide reasonable timelines in which to respond; for the latter, it assures them they all will get an answer. Even more, the procedure can help the superintendent plan for the future. Information that has to be developed by staff should only be made to the superintendent by the board corporate.

* JUST A THOUGHT !

A pattern of requests for information from school board members can be a signboard to a potential issue.

41

Snapshot #16:
The Non-education Issue

Irene is a senior citizen school board member. She has reached her "golden" years and is reaping some of the benefits, such as cheaper movie tickets, discount hotel rooms, an extra 10 per cent off anything she buys at the local mall on "senior" days, and Medicare. She has a prescription drug plan through the school district's health insurance program but she knows that she is fortunate because, almost daily, a friend, family member or constituent laments about the high cost of prescription drugs. Irene is determined to use her platform as a public figure to urge Congress to do more. At the next board meeting she proposes that the school board adopt a resolution urging Congressional action. Her hope is that other school boards across the nation will do the same. Her fellow board members agree that drug costs are a major national problem, but to her surprise and irritation, they disagree that the board should pass a resolution. They turn Irene down despite her warnings that "Someday, you too, could face this problem." What should Irene do?

At school board meetings, keep the focus on education issues.

There's a place for activism for every issue; find the right address.

Tip : The role of a school board is to set school district policy, not national policy. Individual members are welcome to pursue personal political issues, but from the school board dais, actions should be confined to those assigned to the board by state statute.

Irene has other advocacy avenues to pursue. She can write letters to the editor, appear on local media speaking as a concerned citizen, not a school board member. She can email her Congressional delegation and those on key Congressional committees. She can ask local clubs and organizations to take action. She can stand in the mall on special senior citizen day, or any other day, and ask people to sign a petition urging Congress to take action.

Snapshot #17:
The Fractious Board

The Quarrelton City School Board is one of the most fractious in the city's history. The five-member board manages to split two to two on every vote, leaving the harried school board chairman to consistently have to break the tie. More than that, the board members spend a good deal of meeting time carping at each other and non-meeting time shooting barbs at each other in the media. The superintendent is harried, staff morale is low, and the community is embarrassed. The biggest losers are the students who are the recipients of most of the board's cantankerous decisions. What should you do?

Tip : Overcoming personality conflicts, which may be fueled by philosophical ones, is a major but not impossible task. Most states have school board associations that offer a variety of workshops to board members to teach them such things as their duties and responsibilities, voting procedures, board protocol, the open government and public records law, the laws affecting personnel and purchasing procedures, collective bargaining if applicable, how to conduct board meetings, place items on the agenda, and how to build consensus. School boards can schedule their own retreats and use them to establish their own meeting rules beyond the usual reliance on Roberts Rules of Order. They can set time limits for speakers, including themselves, the selection or election of the board chairman, the rules for having cordial and relevant discussions, the timely delivery of agenda materials, and the protocol for establishing and handling consent agendas.

Look to the chairman for leadership. A strong chairman, who is firm yet fair, and who lets everyone express an opinion and doesn't dominate, and who keeps his or her temper and blood pressure under control, may not create a school board "love in" but certainly can produce an atmosphere for reasonable debate and decision.

* JUST A THOUGHT !
Being a school board member means serving the public, not skewering your enemy.

> **Special training for school board members can lead to more constructive and cordial school board meetings.**

> **Board members can agree to disagree, but once the vote is over, they need to jump on the train and ride down the track together.**

Snapshot #18:

The Unprepared School Board Member

Dennis is a school board member who has something to say about every single agenda item that comes before the board, even if it is just a routine item. It is obvious to his fellow board members that though Dennis receives all the information for each item well ahead of the meeting date, he doesn't do his homework. Not only does he have a comment about every issue, Dennis asks questions, which were answered in the material he received in advance of the meeting.

It's easy to tell when a school board member isn't prepared. The evidence is in the types of questions asked and the "off-base" comments that are made. Although his fellow board members would like to tell Dennis to stop talking so much and read his material, they really don't want to antagonize him. What should they do?

Tip :

A better way is to respond to Dennis's questions is by calling his attention to the back-up material and the page containing the relevant information. It could be a slow learning process, but eventually Dennis may get the message.

Be prepared for board meetings and workshops. It's obvious and unfair to your constituents and your colleagues when you are not.

You may think asking countless questions shows that you are inquisitive and diligent. Your audience may just think you are unprepared and incompetent.

Snapshot #19:

The Chatty Cathy Board Member

Chatty Cathy is a different kind of school board member. She reads all her agenda material in advance of the meeting, takes the time to call staff and get her questions answered beforehand, and arms herself with lots of information. At the board meetings, she is ready and able to talk on any and every issue and she does. She quotes research studies and expounds on her philosophies. She gives anecdotal examples to support her positions and rattles on about her visits to schools and meetings with community groups. Long monologues are her favorite form of communication. Getting Cathy to give her vocal chords a periodic rest at board meetings is a challenge, but not impossible. What should you do?

Tip : Adopt a board rule that says every member can speak to every agenda item, but set a time limit of two to three minutes or less. If the board is dealing with a particularly hot item, it always can vote to extend the time limit. Don't expect Cathy to instantly curb her chatty ways but, after time has been called on her repeatedly, she eventually may get the message.

JUST A THOUGHT !
Speak judiciously but carry a big vote.

Control school board meetings by setting time limits for members to speak to agenda items.

Just because you have an opinion, doesn't mean you have to express it.

Snapshot #20: The Grandstander

After winning her first election, Lucy is like a runaway train bearing down on school reform. She is full of excitement, enthusiasm, and ideas on how to improve the reading program, streamline the purchasing practices, attract better teachers, and fix the budget shortfall. Lucy's penchant is to grandstand at all the school board meetings and tell the superintendent how to run the district. In fact, if there were a statewide contest on micro-managing, Lucy would win the blue ribbon. What should she do?

Tip: Lucy's mind is ripe with good ideas, but it also has large pockets of misinformation or no information at all. As a new school board member, she needs to take a deep breath, learn all she can about the school district, and then decide where she wants to devote her reform energy. Most important, she needs to stop grandstanding. Running a good school district is a team effort of the board, which sets good policies, and the superintendent and staff who effectively implement them. Lucy's worthy ideas won't have a chance if everyone around her secretly is wishing she would just stop talking and disappear.

The school board is a "team." Pinpoint the issues that are most important to you and get the others to help you.

Examine the cracks in the image before getting overly impressed with what you see in the mirror.

* JUST A THOUGHT! You cannot be all things to all people. There are just too many of both.

46

Notes: _____

_____

_____

_____

_____

_____

_____

_____

_____

Chapter Three

Heart Healthy Relationships: Keeping Families and Friends Close

"The supreme happiness in life is the conviction that we are loved—loved for ourselves, or rather, loved in spite of ourselves."

Victor Hugo

Snapshot #21:

The Public vs. Private Life Balancing Act

Frances has been on the school board for six months. She is a very conscientious board member and tries never to miss a school board meeting or activity. However, the board's next official meeting is on the same afternoon as her teenage daughter's piano recital. Frances is torn. There are some major issues on the next board agenda and she wants to be there to discuss them and vote. However, the recital is important to her daughter and the teenager will be disappointed if her mother does not attend. What should she do?

Tip:

Parents who spend time with their children are making a value statement.

Keep family matters at the top of your priority list.

* JUST A THOUGHT !
Celebrity status can be a mindset. Yours may be the only mind in which it is set.

The first rule of board membership is "Families First." Although Frances' attendance at the board meeting is significant, it should take second place to her daughter's recital. Frances should check the agenda and see if it is possible to split her time between the meeting and the recital, perhaps leaving the board meeting temporarily to listen to her daughter perform, and then returning to the meeting. She could ask that, as a courtesy to her, consideration of particular items be delayed to a certain time or moved up on the agenda. Hopefully, Frances has accommodated similar requests from her colleagues in the past and they are ready to reciprocate. School board meetings are important; the decisions made at them affect hundreds of students. But there will always be another board meeting. Special events in your children's lives rarely have repeat performances. Take the time to share them.

Snapshot #22:

Focus on Friendships

Tip : Be aware that even though you feel you have time for old friends, the old friends may not feel you have time for them now that you are busy on the school board. Sometimes friends view you as having a different status as an elected official and they build a fence around you. It's not that they stop caring; it is that they think you are too busy and too involved in other things and they hesitate to intrude on your time. Don't let your friends build that "fence." Take the time to call them and remind them you are the same person you were before becoming an elected official and that their friendship is more important than ever. Tell them that while your new schedule may make it more difficult for you to get together as often as before, it doesn't mean that you want to lose touch.

Jill and Pat were good friends who did a lot of things together. They saw each other several times a week, swapped children's stories over the telephone, and strolled the shopping malls when time permitted. When Jill ran for the school board, Pat worked in her campaign. After Jill was elected, she and Pat began to drift apart. Jill was busy with her school board activities; Pat called regularly, then occasionally, and then barely. She perceived Jill more as a busy "elected official" than as a close friend. What should Jill do?

While you are busy educating children, don't forget to embrace your friends.

Build fences around houses not around yourself.

51

Snapshot #23:

Emphasizing the "Significant" in Significant Other

Can school board members remain happily married? This is not material for a new reality television show, but it is a part of public life that needs its own brand of attention. At social functions and elsewhere, the tendency is for people to focus on the elected official and give only perfunctory attention to the other half of the couple. What should you do?

Tip: Curb that tendency. Before conversations swing into full gear, make sure you introduce your spouse and then continually draw him or her into the conversation. Do the "we" thing, the "What do you think, dear?" thing, and the "Did you know that, dear?" thing as much as possible in your conversation. Plan ahead for those invitations to special dinners and formal events requesting your presence as a board member. Respond to the invitation that you will need two tickets; then tell your spouse that both of you have been invited. Make sure you arrange for both of you to have nametags waiting. A neatly pre-printed, correctly spelled nametag is much more welcoming than a hastily scrawled handwritten one that seems to say: "So who invited you?"

> *Don't get over-impressed with yourself; focus on the impression that you make on others.*

> *If you tangoed your way to elected office, don't forget your dance partner.*

Snapshot #24:
Tying the Family Knot

Forget those intimate dinners out alone with your spouse or those special mall trips just with your teenage daughter. Interruptions seem to be inevitable. As a school board member, you can't seem to go to a restaurant, the neighborhood grocery, or a local department store without bumping into someone who wants to talk to you about school "stuff." The problem is: your family wants to be with you, too, and not necessarily while you are deep into "school talk" conversations. What should you do?

Tip : Being a school board member can be a full-time job. Your constituents and official duties can consume every ounce of your time and energy, if you let them. Don't forget the folks nearest and dearest to you who helped you achieve the success you are enjoying. It is not unusual for new school board members to discover that the excitement and pressure of their new role is causing resentment among family members who are beginning to feel neglected. Make time for your family. Call your spouse in the middle of the afternoon and make a date to go somewhere together. Give up local restaurants and steer away from your neighborhood or go out of town when you want that intimate evening alone. Plan a weekend away from home. Check into a hotel at the beach, in the mountains, at the lake, or in a nearby city. Go someplace with just your spouse, or with other family members, so you can have some "time out" to focus on each other.

Families are medieval in nature. They can fight and argue among themselves over an issue, but when the whole world seems to turn against you over some controversial education issue, families tend to pull up the drawbridge and unite to defend you.

> **Families are the anchors in the storms of political life.**

> **The only true "First Family" is your own.**

Snapshot #25:
A Friend Wants a Job

Nancy and her husband, Dan, are long-time members of your monthly bridge club. Their children have gone off to college and Nancy suddenly is faced with the "empty nest" syndrome. Fortunately, as a former teacher, she has been smart enough to keep her teaching certificate current. One Saturday night, while you are in the kitchen getting coffee for the group, Nancy comes in to help. She tells you she wants to return to teaching and asks you to help get her a job. After all, you are her friend. Nancy may be the best bridge player in the world, or the worst. Ditto for her teaching abilities, but she is your friend and you feel obligated. What should you do?

Tip: Tell Nancy to submit a job application to the school district and to make sure all the necessary papers are filed and in order, including her college transcript. Offer to have a set of application papers sent to her home. That way, you will feel you have done something. Tell her to let you know when all her papers have been appropriately completed and submitted and you will have a personnel officer contact her. Call the superintendent and ask that, minimally, Nancy be interviewed. You've helped Nancy. If she gets the job, it means she was qualified and she will feel good about her situation. If she doesn't, it could mean she makes a great friend, but not a qualified teacher. It also could mean you will have to find another fourth for bridge.

The key words are "based upon the superintendent's recommendation" when describing the school board's role to hire, fire, and discipline personnel.

Don't confuse "personal" with "personnel."

Notes:

Chapter Four

The Parent Connection

"Courage is the ladder
on which all the other
virtues mount."
Claire Booth Luce

Snapshot #26:

An Angry Parent

An angry parent calls Clara, a member of the school board, to complain that her son, a ninth grader, has unfairly received an "F" on his science project, which had accidentally been damaged on the school bus. The parent is objecting to the grade and wants the school board member to get it changed. What should Clara do?

Tip : Clara must immediately take control of the situation by not allowing the parent to rattle on and on about how unfair the teacher is and interpreting Clara's willingness to listen as a sign of agreement. She should determine if the parent has talked to her son's teacher and if that didn't work, with the school principal along with the teacher. If those steps have been unsuccessfully taken, Clara can offer to ask the superintendent to assign a staff member to look into the situation. Clara's role as a school board member is to help point the parent in the right direction to have the complaint reviewed, not to step in and demand the grade be changed.

The responsibility of school boards is to set grading policies, not give or change grades.

Knowing you are not the right person to handle a constituent's problem is half the battle; knowing how to direct a constituent to the right person is the other half.

* JUST A THOUGHT !
Never promise anyone that you will fix or change something, only that you will do what you can.

Snapshot #27:

The Missing Math Books

Cindy is a school board member in a small community where having an unlisted home telephone number would be considered an affront to her many neighbors, friends, and constituents. As a result, Cindy's phone rings often. This particular caller wants to know why, with the term half over, fifth grade students at the nearby elementary school still have not received their math books, particularly since the school board has a policy that every student shall have a textbook. Cindy doesn't know why the books haven't arrived. In fact, she didn't even know they hadn't. What should she do?

Tip : Cindy has a choice. She can try to fake the answer and blame it on some vague purchasing delay or she can tell the caller that she is not sure what has caused the delay, but will find out and either return the call during the workday or have a staff member call with the information. When questions come to you and you are at home or anywhere where the answer is not readily available, don't fake it. Tell the person you appreciate hearing about the problem and promise to deliver a response as soon as you know the right answer. Inform the superintendent of the problem and ask him for an explanation.

When you don't know something, don't fake it. Admit you don't know, then make a point of finding out.

Know what you know, not what you think you know.

Snapshot #28:

Fielding Complaints

You are in a hurry to get to a meeting, but you have to make a quick stop to buy gas. A car pulls up to the other side of the pump; the driver gets out, pops open her car's gas cap, and begins fueling. Across the pump, you recognize each other and nod "hello." It's just the opening the other driver wants. She begins to talk to you about her child's personal problem at school. You are only half-listening. You try to think of an appropriate response that will indicate at least a modicum of interest on your part, yet not hinder your rapid getaway. What should you do?

Tip : Don't fall into the instant problem-solving trap, particularly when your mind is clouded with gas fumes and your watch is ticking away. Tell the other driver that you would like to hear more about the issue when you both have time to sit down and talk about it unhurriedly. Give her your telephone number and ask her to call you to set up a good time to meet. That way you can write down all the facts, look into the situation, talk to appropriate staff members, understand the problem from all sides, and then take steps to resolve it.

Don't commit to anything or anyone until you have all the facts.

Instant coffee is okay; instant problem solving is not.

Snapshot #29:

A Parent Demands a Transfer to an Overcrowded School

Mary Ellen has received a call from a parent who wants help in getting her daughter transferred to a different school. Her daughter is being harassed by other students on her way to and from school. It is affecting her schoolwork and causing problems at home. Unfortunately, the school the mother is requesting is overcrowded and not accepting any new students. Mary Ellen suggests an alternate school, but the parent isn't interested. She has "heard" things about the school being offered and doesn't want her child attending it. She wants the school she wants. What should Mary Ellen do?

Tip : Mary Ellen can take another approach. She can invite one or both parents to come with her to visit some other less crowded schools she is recommending. Mary Ellen literally can take the parent by the hand to see, firsthand, what the less crowded schools have to offer. The "up front and personal" approach to selecting a school can be a positive eye-opener for parents and convince them there are other good choices.

> *Use visits to school sites as a marketing tool.*

> *Sometimes a first-hand look can elevate a second-hand choice.*

61

Snapshot #30:

When You Have the Question, But Not the Answer

You are lost in thought in the grocery store trying to decide if you should buy the large, giant, or super size box of cereal. A parent recognizes you as a school board member and asks you a question about the school system. You don't know the answer, but you feel that, as the policy-maker for the school district, you should know just about everything. What should you do?

Tip: Don't try to answer what you don't know. If you are not sure of the answer, be honest and admit it, but write down the person's telephone number and assure the person that you will either follow-up yourself or have a staff member call with the requested information.

> **You are not a repository for all truths. Know your limits.**

> **You're not a panelist on Jeopardy. When you don't know, don't guess.**

Snapshot #31:

A Parent Complains About Excessive Homework

A parent calls you at home to complain about the excessive amount of homework his child is assigned every day. This is the 10th call you have received at home just this evening from parents airing this complaint. In the past few weeks, you have heard the same story at least 30 times. You are tired of hearing it. You know all about the amount of homework the teacher routinely assigns and the difficulty students have completing it. To make matters more frustrating, you are in the middle of dinner when the latest call disturbs you and you are annoyed at the interruption. Your inclination is to cut the caller short and brusquely inform him you've heard this complaint repeatedly and already are looking into it. What should you do?

Tip : Even if it is the 100th call about the same issue, give the caller an attentive ear. Every parent genuinely believes that his child is the most important one in the world. Listen to the story and respond as if this were the first time you have heard about the problem no matter how many times you may have heard it before.

The most important child in the school is the one whose parent is talking to you at that moment.

The parent is the child's first teacher.

Snapshot #32:

Getting to Know You

O ne of Jackie's constituents has contacted her asking to schedule a meeting to discuss a specific problem at her child's school. She does not want to talk about it over the telephone. What should Jackie do?

Tip : Jackie might consider offering to meet the parent for breakfast, lunch, or just a cup of coffee. Conversation tends to be more intimate and open when it takes place in an informal, social setting plus it has a side benefit. Meeting people in social settings is a great way to build new relationships. People have a tendency to "isolate" their elected officials; conversely, the office-holders themselves find it easy to fall into a pattern of spending much of their time with other elected officials or with people who view them as a "business" opportunity. Jackie's reaching out to build new relationships will pay off in many ways. It will expand her circle of friends. It could build future votes. It could create one more satisfied customer. It also could mean more people will send her homemade cookies at holiday time.

The more people you meet, the more you know and the more who know you. Be a people person.

It's good to have acquaintances; it's better to have friends.

Notes: _____

_____

_____

_____

_____

_____

_____

_____

_____

Chapter Five

Staff Stuff:
Working With Principals, Administrators, and Teachers

"A positive attitude may not solve all your problems, but it will annoy enough people to make it worth the effort."
Herman Albright

Snapshot #33:

The Teachers Want Support for More Planning Time

Today's school board meeting includes an agenda item proposing that elementary schools be authorized to send students home an hour early one day a week so teachers have more time to plan. Several teachers have contacted you asking for your support of the item. You listen attentively to their viewpoints, but you are reluctant to commit one way or another until you hear the board discussion. What should you do?

Tip : Be careful how you respond to these requests for support. Try not to say: "That's a wonderful idea," because it indicates support for the item. Similarly, don't say you "love the idea." Love quickly can be translated into a "yes." "Love" your dog, not an idea. Tell the teachers you will "look at the item carefully," and "give it every consideration." By choosing your response thoughtfully, you will leave yourself the option of changing your mind after hearing the board discuss the issue, yet not create more hard feelings because your use of certain words led to mistaken conclusions that you supported the teachers' position.

> *Respond to an idea in a way that does not automatically translate into support for that idea.*

> *Using the term "love" when responding to someone's idea sounds like a commitment of support. "Love" your dog; "consider" an idea.*

Snapshot #34:

The Teacher's Evaluation

You are contacted by a high school teacher who also happens to be a longtime friend. He is very agitated because his principal has given him a satisfactory evaluation, which is one step below the excellent evaluation he anticipated receiving. He doesn't know quite what he wants you to do about his evaluation, but he wants you to do "something." What should you do?

Tip: Board members are not the personnel office, so although you personally may agree the satisfactory evaluation was not good enough, it is not your job to get it changed. Suggest the teacher put his complaint in a letter to the principal with a copy to you. Putting it in writing may give the teacher time to think through the situation and realize what he didn't do to rate the top evaluation. It also may give him time to calm down and decide to take responsibility for the events behind the evaluation. One thing you can't do is agree to step in and fix things. If you mistakenly get on that track, you will find you are not running the district at all; the district is running you.

SPECIAL NOTE: If your district has collective bargaining, chances are the employee contract will contain a formal grievance procedure, which must be followed. In some districts, where collective bargaining is not required, school board rules provide the formal process.

> *A board member's purview includes setting policy not making personnel decisions.*

> *Consider that as a school board member, if you could "fix" everything, what would plumbers and electricians do?*

Snapshot #35:

A Social Interlude Becomes a Complaint Session

At a luncheon for the Principal of the Year, you are seated next to a middle school principal who you have met briefly on other occasions, but who now seems to consider you one of his closest confidants. Between the still partially frozen "fresh" fruit cup and the chicken dijon, he whips out his official mental list of "Complaints Against the Administration" and starts ticking them off one-by-one. What should you do?

Tip : Social events are not conducive to handling complaints. You are relaxed, anxious to have a nice time, and probably not armed with enough facts to resolve anything. However, you want to be understanding and sympathetic, particularly if you sense the complaints may have some validity. Give the principal your telephone number and suggest some possible times when it would be convenient for him to call you to discuss his concerns or to set up an appointment to air them in person. Curtail the conversation by turning your attention to your food. If the main course hasn't arrived, but dessert is on the table eat it. People will admire you for being a non-conformist.

Hear complaints during social hours, but validate and address them during business hours.

At social functions, tackle the salad and steak, but save the complaint du jour for another time and place.

Snapshot #36:
The Staff Story Changes

You have met privately with a school district staff member who has briefed you as to why Spring Creek Elementary, scheduled to be finished two months ago, still isn't finished after being under construction for 18 months. You are satisfied with the answers and intend to repeat the question at the board meeting so parents, too, will know the reasons. To your annoyance and chagrin, when you ask the same questions of the same staff member at the board meeting, the answers are different. You are angry and frustrated. You want to assume a Perry Mason persona and start rapidly firing clever and accusatory questions at the staff member. You want retaliation for appearing to be unprepared. What should you do?

Resolve problems with staff members behind closed doors, not publicly. Being adversarial is non-productive.

* JUST A THOUGHT!
Sideline Staff
Sabotage.

Don't embarrass staff members in public. You will reap what you sow.

Tip : While you may have the right to exercise your board authority, common sense tells you not to do it in such a way that the staff member will never be your ally. If you embarrass him publicly, he may decide to "skew" or "sift" all the future information you need. Save the courtroom-style attack and tongue-lashings for a more private arena. Arrange another private meeting with the staff member. For now, ask to table the agenda item until you are sure you have all the correct information. If you are getting mixed messages from staff, assume the public is too and that your district has a serious problem. Air this problem with your superintendent and have a system developed through which board members can request and receive accurate information in a timely manner.

Snapshot #37: A Teacher Complaint

At a luncheon for the United Fund, you are about to carefully pick up a succulent stuffed shrimp when a teacher you know throws a body block between you and the food table. You try to do an end run around her, but she is determined to get your attention. What should you do?

Tip: Listen to what the teacher has to say. The problem is in her science lab where the hot water faucet runs only cold water. Her students need access to hot water to perform their experiments. She can't seem to get anyone to fix it. Don't promise the teacher you will get it fixed, but do assure her you will look into it. Contact the superintendent and request that he have a staff member follow up on the teacher's concern and to keep you apprised of the progress in resolving the situation. If similar complaints keep coming to you and they seem authentic, ask the superintendent to review the district's maintenance procedures. At the luncheon, thank the teacher for bringing the problem to your attention. Then reward yourself for giving her your full attention. Grab two stuffed shrimp instead of one.

> *When you are presented with a problem; promise to investigate it, but don't promise to fix it.*

> *A "maybe" leaves you room to breathe; a "promise" can choke you.*

JUST A THOUGHT! Be a part of the solution, not a part of the problem.

72

Snapshot #38:

The Administrator Wants a Job Transfer

A mid-level manager finds out there is a job opening in another department for which she feels well qualified. She wants the job. She calls you for help in getting her transfer. What should you do?

Tip : It is only human nature for school board members to want to be Fairy Godmothers or Fathers, wave a magic wand, and grant the person's wish. Put that wand away! Stay away from personnel matters, except those that are part of your school board meeting agenda items. Personnel decisions generally are the prerogative of the superintendent. If you intend to hold the superintendent responsible for the operations of the school district, then let him do his job. If you insist on being the good guy or gal, and you believe the person asking for your help is qualified, offer to let your name be used as a reference. If you are absolutely sure the person could be right for the job, ask the personnel officer to at least grant an interview.

You are not the superintendent or the personnel director; don't try to be.

Snapshot #39:

The Unhappy Job Seeker

You are receiving a daily phone call from an irate teacher who cannot understand why the school district has not offered him a job. He tells you he is appropriately certified and attended your school district's recent job fair where he was interviewed by eight different principals. He hasn't heard anything since then. What should you do?

Tip : The school district needs more teachers and has been on a major recruiting mission both locally and at various colleges and universities. You cannot understand why the district has not offered this teacher a position. Your first inclination is to call the personnel office and demand answers. You ignore that first thought and take the correct step. You send the candidate's name to the personnel office and ask that office to respond to the caller and to advise you why there has been no follow-up. The personnel staff gives you a different slant on the story. In fact, there has been a follow-up call to the candidate basically thanking him for attending the job fair, but not offering him a contract. All but one of the eight interviewers at the job fair gave the candidate the lowest possible rating. Further, the personnel office tells you that the candidate has called every board member and the superintendent every day asking for the contract, even though he has been told that none will be forthcoming. You are glad you followed proper procedures.

A board's employment list is very short. It includes the appointed superintendent, the school board attorney, and in some school districts, an auditor to report directly to the board. Beyond that, the employment function is not your job.

Keep your personnel hat in the closet. It's not proper attire for a school board member.

Snapshot #40:
The Faculty Feud

Sara, a teacher, calls you at home one evening. She is apologetic about calling you at home and seemingly reluctant to divulge the nature of her call. Finally, she tells you that her principal is impossible. He is dictatorial, inept, and unreasonable. He is destroying school morale, making it impossible for her to do her job appropriately and causing stress in her marriage because she is taking her problems home every night. She wants the principal transferred. What should you do?

Tip : Listen to Sara sympathetically and suggest she make a written record of her complaint, copy you, and take it to the next administrative level. Tell her it is important to have accurate data on file, not just anecdotal "he said, she said" material that can't be substantiated. If your district has a labor contract with a formal grievance procedure in it, refer the teacher to those procedures. If not, there may be school board rules governing grievance procedures. Often you will find that if a complaint can't be substantiated in writing, it is being exaggerated. Ask the teacher if there are similar complaints among the school staff, which could be put in writing. If you see a pattern, ask the superintendent to direct you to the appropriate administrator to look into the situation. Tread carefully. There may be a problem that needs to be resolved. On the other hand, it could be a school's internal "family" squabble and you know how families quit fighting and suddenly unite when an "outsider" intrudes.

Allow internal staff disputes to be processed administratively without your interference.

Before you get involved, remember even the Hatfields and McCoys finally declared peace.

*** JUST A THOUGHT !** Stay above school faculty disputes; you could become the fresh kill.

Snapshot #41: The School Rumor

A parent calls you concerned that he has heard a rumor the principal of his child's school is going to be transferred. Even though the school has some problems, the principal is popular with his staff and parents. The idea that he may be leaving is upsetting to them. What should you do?

Tip: Thank the parent for telling you about the rumor, but don't make any commitments regarding the principal's future at the school. Rumors have a built-in communication system that defies the speed of gravity. They fly from mouth to ear, mouth to ear with amazing rapidity, unburdened by any printed verification such as a memorandum, report, or power point presentation. They can be disruptive and divisive and should quickly be squashed. Find out if there is any truth to the rumor. Ask the superintendent to notify the faculty if the rumor isn't true. Contact the parent and elicit his help in talking to other parents. Suggest the principal talk to the faculty and parents. If the rumor is true, ask the superintendent to talk to the faculty or to assign an appropriate staff member to follow through and handle the situation for you.

Rumors are definitely not one of education's three "R's."

Before you act on a rumor, take steps to find out if it is true. If it isn't, follow protocol to put it to rest.

Notes: _____

Chapter Six

Money Matters: Dealing With Budget Decisions

"Facts do not cease
to exist because they
are ignored."
Aldous Huxley

Snapshot #42: The Budget Debate

The Rock Bottom City School District has been quibbling for hours over its proposed budget for the next school year. Contrary to what onlookers may have anticipated, the members haven't been at odds over the bulk of the $32,000,000 operating budget. The board gave a perfunctory nod to that part of the proposal, which essentially took most of its resources to pay for the obvious, including staff salaries, materials, supplies, and school maintenance. It's the last $320,000, only about one percent of the total budget, upon which the board can't agree. Each member is urging the others to allocate the dollars to what he or she considers an essential project. The list includes more school nurses, improving art education, expanding the bilingual education program, or supporting field trips for disadvantaged students. As the quibbling grows more heated and the hours drag on, it is clear the members are ready to go to war for their respective pet projects and have forgotten the district's overall mission statement. What should they do?

> *A school board only is as effective as the sum of its members.*

> *It is impossible to be an effective board member if you are constantly keeping an eye on your next election.*

Tip: Not unlike school boards across the country, Rock Bottom has infinite needs and finite resources. The board needs to take a brief respite and return to its debate with less passionate heads. Knowing they can't do it all, the members need to ask some questions. Can the remaining funds be divided among two or three programs? Where does each program fit into the school board's mission statement? Which program, if any, has the greatest possibility of improving student achievement? Which could reach the most students or perhaps the most in need? Is there a possibility the superintendent could review all other programs and sacrifice or shave some in order to fund some of those under discussion? Couldn't one, two, or all of the programs be put on hold until the financial picture improves?

Simple Advice for Addressing the Not-So-Simple Budget Process

You don't have to be a financial wizard to be an effective school board member, but you do need to understand that developing the school district's annual budget is the most important job you have. While you don't have to know all the details and intricacies of the district budget, you do need to understand some of its rudiments so you can make rationale and defensible decisions and use the budget as your major tool in forwarding the school district's mission.

Get the big budget picture

You should know where the district gets its money, i.e. local, state, and federal funds, and what restrictions each source may dictate regarding how the money can be spent. You should be aware that all money is not alike. Budgets have separate parts, the most common is the portion designated for the day-to-day operation of the schools as opposed to the one earmarked for school facilities (capital outlay). Very often, there are other dollars allocated for specific programs or uses such as textbooks and other instructional materials, school transportation, and school safety, to cite a few examples. Laws and regulations often prohibit the school board from marrying the funds or using them for other than their designated purpose. The result is that there are occasions when you could find yourself defending a decision against giving a salary increase while simultaneously explaining why there is so much money available in your capital outlay fund.

Be aware of the difference between "non-recurring" and "recurring" funds. The former are one-time dollars that probably won't be available for continuing annual expenses. For example: it's not a good idea to increase salaries using non-recurring funds because, as the title indicates, if they don't recur the following year you have dug a huge financial hole for your school district. Better to use "recurring" funds for those expenses that you know will be around every year.

Vote your rhetoric

You campaigned on the promise of improving education. Now focus your budget votes on the district-wide objectives that will reflect your campaign commitment and zeal for improving the basic educational program. Favorite pet projects which you may desperately want to support—and which may be very worthwhile—should take a back seat to the district's overall mission of teaching and learning and should be funded in addition to this mission, not at its expense.

Strategic planning and comprehensive workshops that identify the district's goals and objectives and strategies for achieving them are invaluable in helping you and your fellow board members make sound budget decisions. Those decisions represent the critical links between the district's strategic objectives and its chances of ultimately achieving them.

Embrace accountability

Ask the superintendent to give you budget updates periodically throughout the year. Compare your district's adopted budget—the things you voted to spend money on—with the actual expenditures. Remember, the budget is a plan to spend money and is a living document. It can continually change, but you need to understand the rationale behind the changes. Welcome audits. In fact, even if other authorities already audit your district budget, you, along with your fellow board members, may want to consider authorizing your own independent audit for the sake of greater accountability and stronger community comfort.

Expect the unexpected

School boards almost never have enough money to do everything they want to do, but even tight budgets need to have some set asides for unanticipated expenses. Be sure your budget has a contingency fund to cover unexpected shortfalls or additional costs brought on by such things as Mother Nature's fury, manmade disasters, or sudden influxes of additional students. With so much to be done in your school district and hardly ever enough funds to do it all, it's hard to relegate some of the dollars to a rainy day fund, but it's better to be safe than sorry.

Snapshot #43:
The Painful Portables

Steven believes that, as a member of the school board, it is his right to call an administrator directly and issue orders. Three weeks before the scheduled opening of the new school year, he contacted the director of facilities and demanded two portable classrooms be added to the campus of an overcrowded school in his residence area. Anxious to please a board member, the director of facilities ordered the work done immediately. His action diverted the portables from a school that had been scheduled to get them. What did he learn?

Tip: Four days before school was to open forty parents showed up at the school board meeting demanding to know what happened to the portables their school had been scheduled to receive. Stephen knew; so did the director of facilities, but the news was a surprise to the rest of the board. Board members angrily questioned why plans for the portable sites had been changed and ruminated aloud what would happen if each of them had asked for their preferred projects to be handled out of turn. The heated discussions, charges, and countercharges that permeated the board room discredited the school board, upset the community, and embarrassed Stephen, who silently worried that his future agenda items might well become fatalities of the board's obvious unhappiness with his actions. It's understandable that, as a board member, Stephen was anxious to respond to his constituents, but it is also important that he keep in mind that the school board's role is to set policy and the administration's role is to administer.

> *Everything that goes around comes around.*

> *Only part of the community may be eligible to vote for you, but all of the community is entitled to be represented by you.*

Snapshot #44:

The Pesky Vendor

One of your major election campaign supporters who also is the president of a small software company contacts you. He knows the school district will be requesting bids on software that will prevent students from accessing unacceptable websites. As a good friend of yours and someone who contributed generously to your campaign, he is sure that you will want to help convince the superintendent and staff that his product is the best for the job. What should you do?

Tip : Tell your supporter that you are interested in learning more about his product and that your goal is to make sure the school district gets the best one. Explain the procedure staff uses to review available software programs and recommend the best to the superintendent for submission to the school board. Offer to set up a meeting with the superintendent, before the bid request is issued, so that your friend can learn exactly what the school district is trying to accomplish with the software program. Avoid advocating for his product. It's not your job and it could have repercussions. Staff will think you are stepping in where you do not belong. Besides, you never know how many more of your campaign workers may have connections to software companies. Staying neutral is the proper—and safest—course.

Listen and learn from vendors, but never agree to anything.

Don't promise if you can't deliver. Your friends will become your enemies and your enemies won't change their minds.

Notes: _____

_____

_____

_____

_____

_____

_____

_____

_____

_____

Notes: _____

Chapter Seven

Constituents' Capers: Handling Those Special Cases

"There are people who, instead of listening to what is being said to them, are already listening to what they are going to say themselves."

Albert Guinon

Snapshot #45: The Angry Public Speaker

Blarney is a retired salesman who is making a career of appearing before the school board at its regular meetings and telling the members just how angry he feels about the job they are doing. Blarney doesn't mince words. He criticizes the superintendent, vilifies the board members, and accuses them of being ill-informed, ill-advised, and purveyors of ill-conceived ideas. Blarney holds nothing back as he snarls his way through his allotted speaking time. Much of what Blarney says is incorrect, but interspersed in his angry rhetoric are some plausible ideas and accurate information. The good stuff, however, is drowned in the delivery system. What should you do?

Tip : Accusations, particularly when they are unfounded, are hard to take. They seem to clamor out for defensive responses. No one likes to be publicly attacked or insulted. It is only natural to want to respond to Blarney's antagonistic public comments, but it's not a good idea. Responding to Blarney's charges is like going to war with the newspaper. The paper never runs out of ink; Blarney will never run out of anger. Trying to explain things to him means engaging him in a conversation that he will be happy to continue as long as you give him the opportunity. A better way is to let Blarney say what he has to say and then go on to the next speaker. This is truly a time when "Silence is Golden."

Give speakers at school board meetings time to vent. Listen attentively, but don't respond or do so briefly. Engaging in a public dialogue only leads to confrontation and longer meetings. Save your response for a more private time.

Silence can send a stronger message than the spoken word.

Snapshot #46:

The Loyal Supporter

Tip: Tell Karl that you will look at his proposal to consider what is reasonable and feasible, and possibly bring an item to the board so it can direct the superintendent to consider doing a feasibility study that looks at the pros and cons of contracting for custodial and maintenance services versus keeping it in-house. Don't make any promises. When Karl and other supporters seek "compensation" for their campaign help, keep in mind that, to be an effective school board member, you cannot perpetually be eyeing the next election. Tomorrow brings a different day, a different issue, and the potential for a different response.

Karl is the owner of the area's largest cleaning and maintenance company. He also was one of your staunchest campaign supporters. He raised funds for you, asked his employees to distribute your campaign signs, and made phone calls on your behalf. Now, he has approached you for support to get the school district to hire his company to clean and maintain your schools instead of using in-house school system employees. You want to support your supporters. You want them to know you appreciated their help in the past and may want it again in the future. You also want them to know their help doesn't mean they can "buy" your vote. What should you do?

Every school district has procedures in place for procuring goods and services. They are your safety valve. Follow them.

Your supporters deserve no more or less than any other citizen: that is respect and access.

* JUST A THOUGHT!
You don't owe yourself or your vote to your supporters. You do owe them your honesty and your best foot forward.

Snapshot #47:

The Lobbyist Seeks a Payback

At a chamber of commerce dinner recognizing outstanding leaders in town, you are seated next to a lobbyist who contributed to your election campaign. Between bites of the familiar rubber chicken, the lobbyist talks nonstop about a client he has who is trying to do business with the school system. You can't seem to steer the conversation in another direction, even though you try. What should you do?

Tip: Explain to the lobbyist that the proper move for him to make would be to talk to the superintendent and appropriate staff and that you would be happy to alert both to expect his call. Suggest he send you some written material about his client so you can be more informed. To politely end the conversation, sacrifice the rubber chicken, get out of your chair, and circulate throughout the room. Work the room diligently, going from table to table, shaking hands, and chatting with people. This action will have multi-benefits: it gets you away from your unwanted dinner companion; it impresses people with your sincerity as you demonstrate that, even though the campaign is over, you still like to stop and talk to them; it helps with personal weight control because it will prevent you from overeating.

> **Using the district's "chain of command" gives you the freedom to lead.**

> **It's okay to owe gratitude, not to owe favors.**

90

Snapshot #48:

The Chronic Complainer

> One way to silence school critics is to encourage them to personally explore the object of their criticism.

> Schools are like movies and books. Until you see or read one, you have to rely on someone else's rating.

Cranky constituents are a challenge. Abigail is a retired nurse with time on her hands and complaints on her mind. Her passion is to whine about the school system and she is an expert at it. She stores her complaints in mental torpedo tubes. While you are busy using your school board knowledge to try and deflect one complaint, she is mentally getting ready to fire the next one. Abigail's view of the school system is that: it has too many administrators; the students don't need computer—books are better; there's no discipline in schools; the superintendent's salary is too high; her tax dollars are being wasted; the Japanese score higher than Americans in every subject. According to Abigail, when she went to school, everything was better, cheaper, and safer. Her memory of school mirrors Garrison Keillor's famous and fictitious "Lake Wobegon," where all the teachers have master's degrees and all the children are above average. It's almost impossible to win the complaint war with Abigail or other chronic education bashers by using logical, rational explanations based on your knowledge as a school board member. What should you do?

Tip : Try the up-front and personal approach. It's been years since Abigail was inside a public school. She has no idea of what goes on: the amount of learning that takes place; the complexities of the projects students produce; the dedication of the staff; the wealth of material in the curriculum. Her view of school largely is based on some negative media story that appeared in yesterday's newspaper. Offer Abigail a "walk on the wild side." Take her by the hand to visit some schools. If necessary, entice her with the offer of a free breakfast or lunch to get her inside the school. Try to arrange for Abigail to attend a school play or student concert. Perhaps some of her peers will attend with her. Student talent never ceases to amaze audiences. At the very most, you may turn Abigail into one of the school district's major supporters. At the very least, she may stop lauding the Japanese schools, which she never has visited either.

Chapter Eight

Community Challenges: Keeping Your Hometown on Your Side

"Get the facts or the facts will get you. And when you get them, get them right, or they will get you wrong."

Dr. Thomas Fuller

Snapshot #49:

The Halloween Celebration Incident

Contrary to what some folks may think, Whitman's, Brachs, Hershey's, and other major candy manufacturers did not start Halloween. In fact, Halloween comes from All Hallows' Day, which started out as a solemn day of remembrance for deceased relatives many centuries ago and is rooted in religious beliefs. Because of this, some members of your community take issue with the annual Halloween costume parade at the high school followed by a huge "Trick or Treat" bonanza in the school cafetorium. They do not want their tax dollars providing the refreshments for this event. They think the event violates the separation of church and state. What should you do?

Tip : Events like Halloween can make school "special" for some, but not for all. You, on the other hand, are the board member for "all." Devise a compromise. Be inventive.

Don your Robin Hood costume and seek financial help from your local organizations and businesses to pay for the event. Almost certainly there will be some who are happy to jump on your parade and provide non-tax dollars for refreshments. Leave out any religious references in the Halloween observance, but go heavy on the candy corn and apple cider.

Be sensitive to the beliefs, views, and feelings of all your constituents.

Being conventional and being creative are not mutually exclusive.

Snapshot #50:

The Schools Won't Open on Time

Lorie's school district is in turmoil. The new school year starts in three days, but her school board has just been informed by the fire marshal that none of the schools can be opened because of fire safety code violations. The fact that most of the violations are not serious and easily could be fixed without disrupting classes doesn't seem to faze the fire marshal. His orders are: safety first; then start school. Parents are furious, the superintendent is harassed, the community is incensed, and the media is adding fuel to the "potential" fire. Students, on the other hand, seem to be cheerfully resigned to the delayed opening. What puzzles and frustrates Lorie and the other school board members is that the district next door has similar fire code violations, but its fire officials agreed that schools could open while repairs are under way. What should Lorie do?

> *The school district's external relations are every bit as important as its internal ones.*

> *Don't look to your community to help you in the tough times, if you shut it out in the good times.*

Tip: While the neighboring district had made it a practice of accepting the local fire marshal's offers of help and advice with fire safety inspections and repairs, Lorie's superintendent and staff routinely turned down such offers. When a new state law decreed that the local fire marshal had authority to inspect schools and shut them down if necessary. Lorie's fire officials saw it as a chance to get even. A school district is not an island unto itself. It's part of the community. School board members, along with the superintendent and staff, need to build relationships with all segments of the community so that when the tough times do come, the district won't be floating alone in its sea of trouble.

95

Snapshot #51:

The Stakeholders' Storm

Time flies; things change. It only was two years ago when a parental storm of protest erupted over the board's decision to house some 700 seventh and eighth grade students in the high school while a new middle school was under construction. Parental objections at that time were cooled by the news that the move would be "temporary" and they could have something to say about where the new school would be located. Now the middle school is ready and parents are protesting again. This time they don't want their students to move out of the high school. They love it! They are upset the superintendent is recommending the board stay with the original plan. What should you do?

Tip : Before you make a final decision, meet with the parents and listen to their concerns. Ask for their suggestions. Offer yours. Come up with a compromise. Maybe the middle school exodus should be carried out in phases over the next two to four years. Parent power may not move mountains, but it certainly can ease the way toward a peaceful middle school move.

An ounce of stakeholder input is worth an army of angry parents.

Major changes and major policy issues deserve major stakeholder input. Don't go it alone. Find out what the community wants, weigh the facts, then vote your conscience.

Snapshot #52:
The Non-Promotion Plan

A bitter battle is swirling in your school district around the board's policy that prohibits promoting fourth grade students who failed their grade level assessment test. Instead, they can attend an intense summer remediation program followed by re-testing. This year, however, the word is out in the community that the teachers are recommending that re-testing apply only to students the teachers think can pass on the second attempt. The others should repeat the fourth grade rather than being subject to another failure. Parents are up in arms. They are incensed that their children won't be given a second chance, based on a teacher's opinion. They believe equity issues are involved. They are appalled at the teachers' defeatist attitude. What should you do?

> *Give the superintendent advance notice that an issue is creating community controversy.*

> *Communities prefer harmony to haranguing at the school board and superintendent level. Good communication can facilitate the former and minimize the latter.*

Tip: Talk to the superintendent and find out the status of the teachers' recommendation. Chances are he has not made a decision on this issue and is planning to bring it to the school board for discussion. Give him a "heads up" that the issue is going to be a hot one when it does come to the board. Warn him that you intend to ask a lot of questions about the proposal and he needs to be prepared to respond. Not warning him puts him at a disadvantage and sends a message of discord to the community. Advance communication enables you to demonstrate to the community that you have heard its concerns and are responding and that the superintendent also is on top of the issue. Whether they agree with every decision or not, communities prefer to see their superintendent and school board working together.

Snapshot #53:
The Community Connections

Your number one goal in running for the school board was to improve student achievement. Once elected, your heart's desire is to work with the superintendent to make sure that the school district evaluates every one of its academic programs to determine if it is the right program for the right group of students. Your intense focus on finding ways to improve student achievement doesn't leave much time for anything else. You did the speech circuit when you were running for office. That's the past. Now you want to spend your time in-house, reforming education. What should you do?

Every village has a leader. In the Education Village, you are one of those leaders.

The more your constituents see of you, the more they feel they are being represented.

Tip : Heed the familiar saying: "It takes a whole village to raise a child" and don't forsake your community. It is your role to get the "village" involved in schools. Accept invitations to talk to all kinds of groups: parents, businesses, and civic organizations; social service agencies and neighborhood clubs. Accept some of those breakfast gigs even if you absolutely hate to get up in the morning. Whether you are able to devote full-time to being a board member or you are meshing your board schedule with your job schedule, you need to be an ambassador for your school district at every opportunity. There may be more invitations than time permits you to accept, but schedule as many as you can. The more events you attend the more your constituents will feel they are being well represented. Use your attendance at these events as opportunities to inform people about what's happening in your schools. Make sure you have all the facts and information and know what you are talking about. Urge your audience to become actively involved in the school district. Offer them a menu of ways to do that such as mentoring, volunteering, tutoring, task force membership, working with the PTA, and whatever else is available.

Snapshot #54:

The Legislative Alliance

Nothing seems to split a person's personality faster than when they run for the state legislature. On the campaign trail, it is all about education being the number one priority and the need to increase teachers' salaries, build more schools, and improve student achievement. Postelection, when the candidate now is a legislator, it becomes a matter of too many administrators, too much tax money being wasted, holding school boards responsible for outcomes, and raising standards. Dealing with legislators is one of the toughest roles in the school board venue. It's also one of the most important. What should you do?

Tip: Get to know your legislators when they are at home in the district, not when you have to travel to the state capitol to meet them. At home, they have time and less pressure and are more inclined to listen. In the capitol, particularly when the legislature is in session, they are being pulled 100 different ways on 100 different issues. They have less time to listen and less patience to listen for a long time. Identify which schools are in each legislator's district. This will vary depending upon the size of your district and the number of legislators in your delegation. Encourage your principals, joined by their parent groups, to invite their respective legislator(s) into their schools. Use those visits as an opportunity to point out any overcrowded situations in the school or the need for more technology. Don't be shy. Point out the good stuff, but also where the school and the school district need help, which usually is more money. When you do get the legislator's attention, get to the point of your meeting quickly; know your facts and be polite. It's fine to disagree with a legislator and press for your position, but no matter how inflexible the lawmaker may seem, don't attack. Urge, beg, argue, cajole, sweet talk, but don't get personal.

> *The legislator who is your biggest foe today on one issue very well could be your staunchest friend tomorrow on a different issue.*

> *Get to know your legislators while they are on the home front. It's a friendlier place.*

Snapshot #55:

The "Elected Officials' Club"

The Homeowners' Association in your neighborhood has decided it wants a community center for the area and has appointed a committee to determine how to get one. The committee chairman contacts you seeking help. After all, you are a member of the community. You also are an elected official involved with children. You are the perfect person to help get this project accomplished. What should you do?

Tip:

Be prepared in advance to help with community issues outside of the school system arena. As an elected official, you have a slightly different status than those who don't hold office. You are a member of what is called the "EOC," the "Elected Officials' Club," which means you have the opportunity to network with other elected officials and associate with them on some sort of a common playing field. Take advantage of the "Club." Establish relationships with legislators, other city and county elected officers, and your congressional representatives. The school board may not be in a position to provide the community center, but there are others in the "EOC" who may be able to point the way.

> *Networking with other elected officials is a win-win situation for the community and the school district.*

> *View every other office holder as an opportunity to enhance your own office.*

Snapshot #56:
The Media Is Not the Enemy

Tip : Building relationships with the press could help alleviate some of its negative focus on you. Make it a point to be up-front and honest with reporters and editors. Respond to their calls and share as much information as you can with them. Don't play favorites by helping one reporter scoop another. There are days when you may not believe it, but the press is people and, like people everywhere, its members respond to honesty, cooperation, and a few sincere questions that tell them you are interested in them as human beings. You may not become the daily darling of the press by building relationships with its members, but you could very well avoid becoming its daily dartboard.

At times it seems the media is always attacking the board either for something it has done or something it is thinking of doing. The attacks appear to focus on some school board members, you among them, to the exclusion of the others. You can't understand why this is happening. While you may not want to party with the press, you do need to partner with it. What should you do?

The bad news is that bad news won't go away. The good news is that some people can't read; some who can won't see the story; some who see it, won't read it; some who read it, won't believe it; and some who believe it are not your friends anyway. *

The news media is not your public relations department. *

* JUST A THOUGHT!
The media has a job to do. With or without you, it will do it.
The media may not be the school board's worst enemy. The board's worst enemy may be itself.

*Source: Florida School Boards Association

Epilogue

"A sense of humor is part of the art of leadership, of getting along with people, of getting things done."
Dwight D. Eisenhower

May you continue your journey of communicating effectively with everyone who crosses your path. The more you practice the tools and techniques provided here, the better communicator you will become. By communicating effectively, you will not only serve your own needs, but you will be better equipped to serve those of your children and family.

We send our best wishes for your continued growth from every communication opportunity that comes your way. We would love to hear from you! How did the book help you, what were your favorite snapshots, and what tips or worksheets did you like best? Please send us your comments.

You can write to us at:

Cheli Cerra
9737 N.W. 41 Street, #356
Miami, FL 33178
Cheli@school-talk.com

Ruth Jacoby
P. O. Box 8405
Coral Springs, FL 33075
DrRuth@school-talk.com

We look forward to effectively communicating with you!

Share Your Snapshots

Your Snapshot

How do you make communication easier?

We invite you to share with us your snapshots. Please let us know what situations you have dealt with, what tools you have developed, and what worksheets you use to make your communications easier. We would love to feature you in our next book.

Please send submissions to:
submissions@school-talk.com

You can also visit the school-talk.com website at **http://www.school-talk.com** or personally email each author at the address below:
Cheli at: Cheli@school-talk.com
Ruth at: DrRuth@school-talk.com

We hope that you have enjoyed reading *School Board Talk!* as much as we have enjoyed writing it.

Appendix A
Toolkit for Success

School Board Assessment

As a school board member you already have successfully crossed the hurdles and pitfalls of running for office. However, there are other potential candidates out there who would appreciate your advice when they are considering running for the school board. Tell the potential candidate to run through the following assessment. It will help determine if he/she "really" wants to run for office. Just for fun, take the assessment yourself to see if the answers you would have given would have influenced your decision to seek office.

☐ How many students are enrolled in the school district?

☐ Is the district growing in student enrollment every year or declining?

☐ How many schools does the school system operate?

☐ How many staff members are employed including teachers, administrators, and support staff?

☐ Are there employee unions with whom the school board must collectively bargain?

☐ Is the superintendent appointed or elected?

☐ Where does the school district get its funding? (State revenue, local taxes, federal dollars)

☐ Are you aware a school board really has only two official duties? (Hire the Superintendent/ Approve the Budget)

☐ Are you comfortable talking to large and small groups?

☐ Can you frame a message and deliver it clearly and succinctly without rambling?

☐ Are you willing to ask people to help fund your campaign? If not, do you have someone you can count on to do that for you?

☐ Are you willing to speak to all kinds of groups: Kiwanis, Chamber of Commerce, Rotary, Homeowners Association's in the morning, afternoon, or evening?

☐ Are you thick-skinned and confident enough to handle negative media comments about you when you take an unpopular stand on an issue?

☐ Does your family support your running for office?

☐ Does your family understand how much time away from home being a school board member requires?

☐ If you are a parent, do your children understand there will be times you may not be able to attend baseball or soccer games or cook dinner for them?

☐ Is your spouse willing to share the public limelight with you?

☐ In general, have you assessed how much time is involved in being a good school board member?

☐ Do you have some idea of the amount of material you will be asked to read and review?

Information Checklist

Here is a partial list of materials and information new board members need to review and have on hand in order to get started and veteran board members need to keep updated and available as ready references.

☐ **The school district's annual budget**
☐ **Copies of relevant state statutes covering your role and responsibilities**
☐ **A copy of your state's open meetings and public records laws**
☐ **The district's goals and strategic plan**
☐ **The district's construction plan**
☐ **The school board's policies**
☐ **A list of all schools with their addresses and principals' names**
☐ **A copy of the district's organization chart**
☐ **A list of district staff members with their telephone numbers**
☐ **A brief description of the function of each of the district's departments**
☐ **A master calendar of scheduled school district and school events**
☐ **A copy of the Student Code of Conduct**
☐ **The board rules for conducting meetings and bringing forward agenda items**
☐ **A copy of the superintendent's contract**
☐ **Copies of collective bargaining contracts, if applicable**
☐ **Miscellaneous printed material**

Communicating With the Media

- ☐ Know what you are talking about.
- ☐ Be careful with careless responses; think thoughts first, vocalize them second.
- ☐ Don't fear silences and pauses; use the time to frame your answers.
- ☐ Answer the question; don't give a speech.
- ☐ Keep answers short; don't let your point get lost in a maze of words.
- ☐ Stay away from jargon; it's a foreign language.
- ☐ Don't say anything you don't want to see in print.
- ☐ Don't talk "off the record"; nothing is off the record.
- ☐ Never say "no comment"; it sounds suspicious.
- ☐ If you don't know, say so and offer to find out.
- ☐ If you know, but can't say, offer other information.
- ☐ Turn negative questions into positive answers.
- ☐ Ignore hypothetical questions; stick to the facts, not fiction.
- ☐ Use your own words; don't let the reporter put his in your mouth.
- ☐ Express your own opinions; don't echo the reporters.
- ☐ Don't lie; if you can't talk about the truth, don't talk.
- ☐ Be accurate; if you are not sure, say so.
- ☐ Get your facts straight; give consistent responses.
- ☐ Be confident; you may not know it all, but you know more than the reporter.

- ☐ Don't ask to review the story before it is printed; it's not going to happen.
- ☐ Don't pick fights with the media; it never runs out of ink or airtime.
- ☐ Don't use words to agitate a controversy; calmly explain your position.
- ☐ Share the praise; turn "me" upside down to "we" for positive stories.
- ☐ Don't be condescending, sarcastic, or flip; quotes can turn on you.
- ☐ Stay aware that what you say may be quoted, so be careful how you say it.
- ☐ Brush off criticisms and misquotes; readers and listeners have short memories.
- ☐ Take time to say "thank you" for the good and accurate stories.

Dress for television:

Leave the large prints, flashy patterns, bold stripes, big hats, and shiny jewelry at home. Wear white or solid pastels, a jacket, a tie or small scarf, your usual eyeglasses.

Suggested Code of Ethics for School Board Members

A SCHOOL BOARD MEMBER SHOULD BE COMMITTED TO:

- Forwarding a high-quality education for every student.
- Standing up for his/her convictions and beliefs.
- Being willing to assume responsibilities.
- Working cooperatively with others.
- Dealing with all school matters in a non-partisan manner and not subordinating the education of children and youth to any partisan principle, group interest, or personal ambition.
- Respecting the confidentiality of privileged information.
- Maintaining an awareness that the strength of the school board is as a board, not as individuals, and refraining from making "out-of-meeting" commitments.
- Being informed about state and federal laws and regulations affecting education.
- Attending school board meetings faithfully.
- Preparing for school board meetings by studying the issues on the agenda in advance in order to make informed decisions about them.
- Willing to conduct school business in open meetings, as required by law, even when the subject is controversial or personal.
- Understanding that the primary function of the school board is to establish the policies by which the schools are to be administered, but that the administration of the educational program and the conduct of school business is the prerogative of the superintendent of schools.
- Willing to learn from association with other school board members from throughout the state and nation.
- Being aware that it is as important for the school board to understand and evaluate the educational program of the district as it is to plan for the business of operating it.
- Guarding vigilantly against even the appearance of a conflict of interest.
- Becoming familiar with the laws governing contracts and purchases as they relate to school board members and taking steps to avoid violating them.

CONTRIBUTED BY:
Karelia Martinez-Carbonell, DPA
Director of Development
Carrollton School of the Sacred Heart
Coconut Grove, Florida

School Directory

School	Address	Principal	Phone/Fax

District Contacts

Name:_____ Office:_____ Home:_____

Cell:_____ Email:_____

Superintendent:_____

Board Members:_____

_____

_____

_____

_____

District Staff:_____

_____

_____

_____

_____

_____

Municipality Officials' Contact Sheet

Name:_____

Office:_____ Home: _____

Cell:_____ Email:_____

Mayor: _____

City Councilman: _____

Name: _____

Office:_____ Home: _____

Cell: _____ Email:_____

Mayor: _____

City Councilman: _____

Gift Disclosure Form

Date	Donor	Description	Value

Media Information

Name	Media	Phone

Monthly Planning Calendar

Day/Date	Time	Event

Monthly Expense Report

Date	Time	Item	Amount

Monthly Event Attendance Record

Date	Time	Event

Monthly Telephone Log

Date	Time	Caller	Subject

Federal/State Legislators' Contact Sheet

Name:_____ Address: _____

Office:_____ Email: _____

U.S. Senators: _____

_____

_____

_____

_____

_____

U.S. Representatives: _____

_____

_____

_____

_____

_____

_____

_____

State Legislators: _____

_____

_____

_____

_____

_____

_____

_____

_____

Appendix B
Acronyms: Interpreting School Lingo

Breaking the Code: A Handy Acronym List

ACT	American College Testing
ADA	Adults with Disabilities Act
AFT	American Federation of Teachers
AIP	Academic Instruction Plan
AP	Advanced Placement
AYP	Annual Yearly Progress
CPT	College Placement Test
DOE	Department of Education
EEOC	Equal Employment Opportunity Commission
ESOL	English for Speakers of Other Languages
ESE	Exceptional Student Education
FRN	Federal Relations Network
GAO	Government Accounting Office
GED	General Educational Development Test/Diploma
GPA	Grade Point Average
HIPPA	Health Insurance Portability and Accountability Act
HSCT	High School Competency Test
IDEA	Individuals with Disabilities Education Act
IEP	Individual Education Plan
LEP	Limited English Proficient

NAACP	National Assn. for the Advancement of Colored People
NACAC	National Assn. for College Admission Counseling
NAEP	National Assessment of Educational Progress
NASSP	National Association of Secondary School Principals
NBPTS	National Board for Professional Teaching Standards
NCLB	No Child Left Behind
NEA	National Education Association
NLRB	National Labor Relations Board
NRT	National Reading Test
NSBA	National School Boards Association
OSHA	Occupational Safety and Health Administration
PTA	Parent-Teachers Association
PSAT	Practice Stanford Achievement Test
SAT	Stanford Achievement Test
SDFS	Safe and Drug-Free Schools Act
TTT	Troops for Teachers Program
QZAB	Quality Zone Academy Bonds

Appendix C
Bringing the Art of Communication to You

A Message from Cheli & Ruth

Thank you for considering one of our breakthrough programs for your personal development. We look forward to having the opportunity to offer you a motivational, thought-provoking, fun program rich in both content and humor. Our list of clients includes parents, teachers, principals, superintendents, and others who want to become effective communicators.

Here's what we want you to know more than anything else . . .

We understand firsthand the freedom that comes with communicating effectively. Like you, we have been there. As parents we have had the "in the trenches" experiences, and we have created a continuum of effective techniques thousands of individuals have used to achieve successful communication. But good communication is an ongoing exercise, and for people to continue to learn and to use the tools we offer, those tools must be easy to access. To that end, we have written the book *School Board Talk! The Art of Effective Communication*, which we can also have available to complement our program.

Learning how to effectively communicate is a necessity. People who know how to communicate well can head off problems before they arise, build strong relationships, create partnerships, and chart a path for their children's success.

Which is a better expenditure of time, money, and effort: constantly having to remedy the problems that result from communication breakdowns, or being able to address difficult situations proactively through skilled communication? The choice is clear: knowing how to communicate effectively is essential, and we can teach you that skill.

Our programs have been tried and tested to provide you with first-class, professional information and materials. You can choose from a wide variety of our proven courses or have us customize one for your needs.

Contact us at http://www.school-talk.com and tell us your communication challenge. We want to help you!

Regards,
Cheli Cerra, M.Ed.
Ruth Jacoby, Ed.D.

Let's Talk!
Learning the Art of Effective Communication

A successful communicator knows his audience and how to get his point across without creating any misunderstandings. In this hands-on, fun, and informative program, you will learn the tools necessary to begin artfully communicating with others. Learn how to:

- **use key words to defuse hostile situations;**
- **listen effectively;**
- **clearly convey your point to get your message heard; and**
- **create positive relationships through effective communication.**

Cheli and Ruth use hands-on, personal experiences and real-life case studies to demonstrate and teach the tools necessary in learning the art of effective communication.

Book this program for your next meeting or convention and let Cheli and Ruth teach the staff within your organization the steps necessary to diffuse hostile situations, learn the art of listening, and create a positive communication-friendly environment.

Communication Blueprint for Success!

In this eye-opening workshop, the presenters will provide the participants with a self-assessment skills test that will reveal their personal communication comfort level. From this self-assessment, the audience will begin to map their own personal blueprint for communication success.

Cheli and Ruth use situations, snapshots, and activities to involve the audience. This interactive workshop is fun and informative. Participants will learn how to:

- **use key phrases to capture attention;**
- **talk effortlessly through difficult communication situations; and**
- **learn the number one secret to effective communication.**

Book this program for yourself today and leave with a personal communication blueprint that you can begin to implement immediately.

Contact us at http://www.school-talk.com

About the Authors

About Cheli Cerra

For more than 18 years, she has helped thousands of children achieve school and life success. As a school principal, and a mother of two, Cheli knows firsthand the issues that teachers, parents, and children face. She was the founding principal of one of the first K-8 schools in Miami-Dade County, Florida, Everglades Elementary. The school of 1,500 students received an "A+" rating from the Florida Department of Education for two consecutive years under Cheli's leadership.

Cheli is the founder of **Eduville.com**, a life-long learning community. Her company provides resources and strategies for parents and teachers to help their children achieve school and life success, as well as continue the love of life-long learning. Among her resources are Smarter Kid Secrets, a free monthly e-zine, and her website **http://www.eduville.com,** full of tips, techniques, and strategies useful for anyone interested in helping a child succeed.

Recognized as **"The Right Choice"** by *Woman's Day Magazine,* and featured on over 30 radio shows throughout the country, Cheli is committed to education. Because of her leadership expertise, Cheli was invited to join twelve other experts in authoring ***Real World Leadership Strategies That Work,*** published by Insight Publishing.

Cheli is committed to helping teachers and parents come together for the success of children. Her seminars, coaching programs, and presentations have provided strategies that empower her audiences to action. She will captivate you by teaching the lessons learned from her in-the-trenches experience in public education. As a wife and working mother of two, she understands the reality of everyday life and creates strategies to meet these challenges quickly and easily. Her powerful message of immigrating to this country, learning the language, and adapting to a new culture, also give Cheli a unique insight to the real-world challenges children face today.

About Dr. Ruth Jacoby

Dr. Ruth is the founding principal of the Somerset Academy charter schools, which include five charter schools with 1,250 students in pre-kindergarten through tenth grade. She has more than 30 years of experience as an administrator and educator, in traditional public, private, and charter schools. Under her leadership, Somerset Charter School became one of the first charter schools to receive SACS (Southern Association of Colleges and Schools) accreditation. Her middle school received an "A+" rating from the Florida Department of Education in its first year of operation.

Dr. Ruth received her Ed.D. degree in Child and Youth Studies for Children from Birth through 18 Years from Nova Southeastern University, and her Masters of Science in Special Needs and Bachelor of Science in Early Childhood and Elementary Education from Brooklyn College.

During the past three years, Dr. Ruth has become actively involved in educating other charter school personnel in how to develop standards-based curriculum and assessments. Her school was one of the founding partners of the Tri-County Charter School Partnership, which has implemented three South Florida Annenberg Challenge grants in student assessment and school accountability and two Florida Charter School Dissemination Grants. She serves on several governing boards for charter schools in Miami-Dade and Broward County, Florida, and is an active member of the Florida Consortium of Charter Schools.

Notes: _____

_____

_____

_____

_____

_____

_____

_____

_____

A very special thanks to the following individuals who collectively contributed
their stories, advice, and counseling gleaned from their experiences
as school board members, experts in the field of public education,
or as talented editors of this book.

Dr. Wayne Blanton
G. Holmes Braddock
Judie Budnick
Paulette Burdick
Thomas A. Cerra
Jeanne Dozier
Mike Eader
Beverly Gallagher
Kathy Hayes
Dr. Jane Kuckel
Dr. James R. Oglesby
Eric J. Parker
Linda Sutherland
Paula Wallace

"Effective communicators always leave a piece of wisdom with their audience."

To your artful and effective communication.

Cheli & Ruth

Let us hear from you . . . send us your snapshots. Email Cheli and Ruth at:

Cheli Cerra
Cheli@school-talk.com

Ruth Jacoby
DrRuth@school-talk.com

Notes: _____

_____

_____

_____

_____

_____

_____

_____

_____

_____

Notes: _____

_____

_____

_____

_____

_____

_____

_____

_____

The *School Talk!* Series
by Cheli Cerra, M.Ed. and Ruth Jacoby, Ed.D.

Parent Talk! The Art of Effective Communication With the School and Your Child

This must-have guide for parents provides 52 "snapshots" of just about every conceivable situation than can arise between a parent, a student, and a school and provides clear, simple suggestions for positive solutions. From "My child's friend is a bad influence" to "I don't understand the results from my child's test," it covers all the typical events in a student's school experience.

ISBN 0-471-72013-5   **Paperback**   **www.josseybass.com**

Teacher Talk! The Art of Effective Communication

"An amazing compilation of what to say to parents. This book is a must have for your professional library."

—*Harry K. Wong, Ed.D., author of the bestselling* The First Days of School

An essential guidebook for all teachers that presents effective strategies for handling 52 common situations and simple ways to communicate with students, parents, and administrators. Features worksheets, checklists, sample letters, and more.

ISBN 0-471-72014-3   **Paperback**   **www.josseybass.com**

Principal Talk! The Art of Effective Communication in Successful School Leadership

Principal Talk! provides simple communication strategies and advice to keep teachers, students, parents, staff, and the community in your corner. A must-read for today's educational leader to be successful in today's reform climate.

—*Jack Canfield, co-author,* Chicken Soup for the Teacher's Soul

This user-friendly, quick reference presents 52 "snapshots" of communication issues faced by busy principals and assistant principals in working with staff, parents, teachers, and the community.

ISBN 0-7879-7911-2   **Paperback**   **www.josseybass.com**

School Board Talk! The Art of Effective Communication

For both the aspiring and the veteran school board members, this book offers tips, worksheets, and practical advice to help board members develop and improve communication skills, survive in political office, and make a difference in education. In its user-friendly, easy-to-browse pages you'll find 50 "snapshots" and solution strategies on topics such as: casting the lone "no" vote and surviving, keeping your family in your fan club, building a school board team, handling constituent calls, and conquering the e-mail and memo mountain.

ISBN 0-7879-7912-0   **Paperback**   **www.josseybass.com**